NEET HELPER

CELL-THE BASIC UNIT OF LIFE

HANAN YOUSUF NAIKOO

ISBN 979-888555632-3

THE WORLD IS SO DARK, AND LIGHT IS PRECIOUS.

COME CLOSER, DEAR READER.

Contents

FOREWORD

This book is written for students of NEET. This is a very fascinating book as it is written short. To the point concepts is the beauty of this book . After thanking Almighty Allah and my family for their endless support, i am thankfull to my teachers for their guidance, reviews and recommendations.Hope the reader will find it enjoying.

HANAN YOUSUF NAIKOO

Acknowledgements

On this ocassion i wish to express my gratitude to all fellow beings and Notion publications.

I

INTRODUCTION TO CELL

- Cell is the basic structural and functional unit of life. It is also called as building block of life.
- A cell is the simplest integrated organisation of living systems, which is csapable of independent survival
- Galilio Galilie invented a microscope named as LITTLE EYE(Magnifying power = 15X)
- Han Jannssen & Zaharias Jannssen invented the first microscope named FLEA LENS(6X-14X)
- The term Microscope was coined by Giovanni Faber
- Robert Hooke in 1665 observed the slices of Oak tree under a microscope of magnifying power 42X and found a hoiney comb like structure. He named the compartments as CELLULA. He observed cell wall.
- th credit for coining the term cell is given to robert hooke.
- Anton Von Leewonhoik observed and describedthe live cells under microscope of magnifying power 240X. he observed Sperms, RBC, Bacteria, Protozoa.
- .Electreon microscope was invented byby Knoll & Ruska.
- Phase Contrast Microscope is used to observe live cells or rocessess like meiosis ans mitosis. it was invented by Fritz Zernike.
- Schleiden (German Botanist 1838) and Schwann(British Zoologist 1839) proposed that plants and animals are made of cells.3

- Schwann formulated the cell hypothesis which states that all living organisms are made of cells and their products.
- "Cell wall is the characteristic feature of plant cells", statement by Schwann.
- Omnis Cellula-e-Cellula i.e, cells arise from pre existing cells by process of cell division (Rudolf virchow 1855).

II

CELL THEORY

- Cell theory was given by Schleiden & Schwann(1838-1839).

POSTULATES

- Cell is the basic unit of life i.e, all living organisms are made of cells.
- Cell is not only a structural unit but is a structural unit but is also a functional unit of life.
- Cell is a mass of protoplasm containing a nucleus nd surrounded by a cell membrane. If it is a plant cell then it may be surrounded by a cell wall.
- According to cell theorey all the cells undergo similar basic metabolic processess.
- The functions of an organism is the sum total of the individual functions of the cells.

LIMITATIONS

- It failed to prove the origin of the cells. Schwann stated that cells arise by a process of crystallisation. He proposed "cell fraction crystallisation theorey". Schleiden stated that cells arise through budding.

- It failed to prove the transmission of characters from one generation to the next generation.Later on Haeckel stated that nucleus of a cell is involved in the transmission of characters from one generation to the next.
- According to cell theorey a cell must possess a nucleus. But RBC's, Sieve tube cells and Prokaryotic cells lack nucleus.Prokaryotic cells instead possess a nucleoid, which contains a circular chromosome called Pro-chromosome. RBC's are secondarily prokaryotic or functinally prokaryotic.
- According to cell theory, a cell possess a single nucleus. In muscle cells, vaucheria and fungi there is a multi nucleate condition.
- According to cell theory all cells must possess a protoplasm.The epidermal cells contain a protein called KERATIN which makes the cells impermeable towards water. Simillarly suberin is present in plant cells.

NOTE

- RBC degenrate its nucleus because of following reasons;

1. Deliver oxygen to cells rather than used by its own organells
2. To create more space inside RBC to accomidate more oxygen
3. To make it shrinkable so that it can pass through capillary

- In animal world multinucleate condition is known as ***synctium*** *(two cells fuse together by dissolving membrane).*
- In plant world multinucleate condition is known as ***coenocyte*** *(karyokinesis not followed by cytokinesis).*

III

CELL DOCTRINE OR CELL PRINCIPLE

The cell theory was redefined or upgraded to form the cell doctrine or cell principle.

POSTULATES

- Cell is the basic or fundamental unit of life i.e all living organisms are made up of cells and their products.
- Cell is not only the structural unit rather it is the unit of function, heridity,reproduction and disease.
- The functions of an organism is the sum total of all the functions of individual cells.
- Cell is the mass of protoplasm containing one or more nuclei and their nuclear products.
- Cell is surrounded by cell membrane which may or may not be surrounded by cell wall.
- Cells do not arise de novo but arise from pre existing cells.
- All cells have similar physical structure, cell composition, and basic ,metabolic functions.
- Cells can survive independently but their organells fail to do do so.
- Every cell possess a complete set of genetic information but they are able to use only a certain part of it due to speciation.

NOTE

- ***CELL = CELL WALL + PROTOPLASM***
- ***PROTOPLASM = CYTOTOPLASM + NUCLEUS***
- ***CYTOPLASM = ORGANELLS + CYTOSOL***
- ***CYTOSOL = CYTOPLASM - ORGANELLS***

POINTS TO PONDER

- ***Dujardin*** **called the living matter of protozoal cell as *sarcode.***
- ***Von Mohl & Purkinje coined the term PROTOPLASM .***
- ***Huxley*** called ***PROTOPLASM*** as 'physical basis of life'.
- Term ***PROTOPLAST was coined by HANSTEIN.***
- Term ***cytoplasm*** was coined by ***strausburger.*** Also known as ***Inter-Mileiu***

IV
PROKARYOTIC CELL

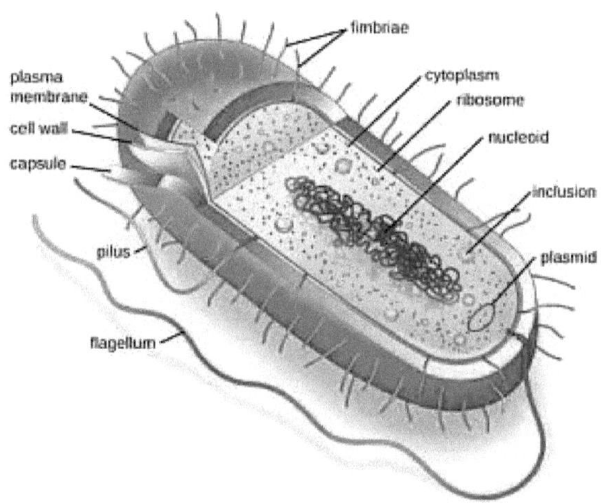

PROKARYOTIC CELL

CHARACTERISTICS

- It contains nucleoid,pro-chromosome/genophore
- Circular DNA
- Lack histones and non histonic proteins but Polyamines are present
- Plasmids are present

- Possess upward foldings of cell membrane called Mesosomes
- Cell wall is made of Peptidoglycines and N-acetyl muramic acid
- Ribosomes are 70s
- Cells have single envelope
- Phagocytosis & Pinocytosis absent
- Appandages are present in the form of fimbrae,pilli & flagella
- Flagella is single stranded
- Flagella is made of protein called flagellin and pilli is made of pillin protein

V

EUKARYOTIC CELL

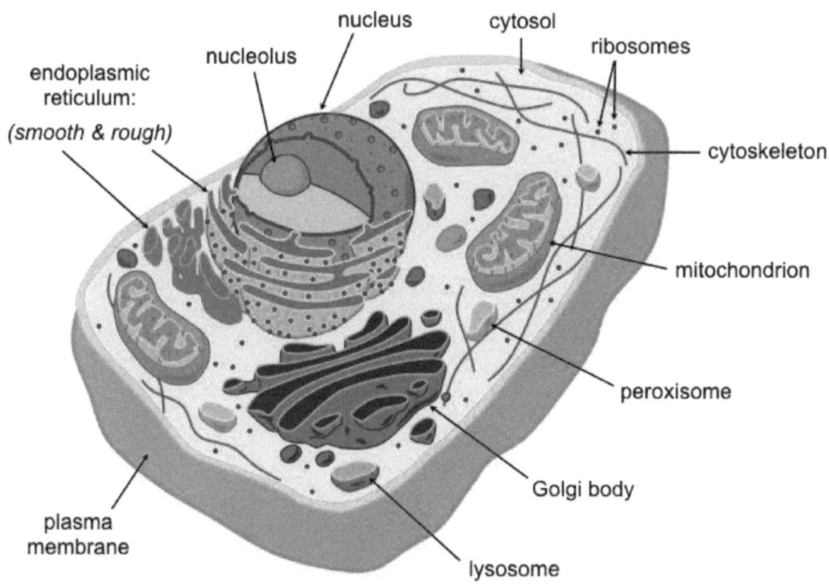

EUKARYOTIC CELL

CHARACTERISTS

- It contains nucleus

- Chromosomes are present
- DNA is linear
- Histones and non Histonic proteins are present
- Plasmids are absent
- Mesosomes are also absent
- Cell membrane is stablised by cholesterol
- Ribosomes are 80s
- Double envelope system present
- Many organells are present
- Phagocytosis and Pinocytosis is seen in animal cell
- Appandages are present in the form of flagella and cilia
- 9+2 arrangement of cilia and flagella
- Flagella and cilia is made of a protein called tubelin

VI

RIBOSOME

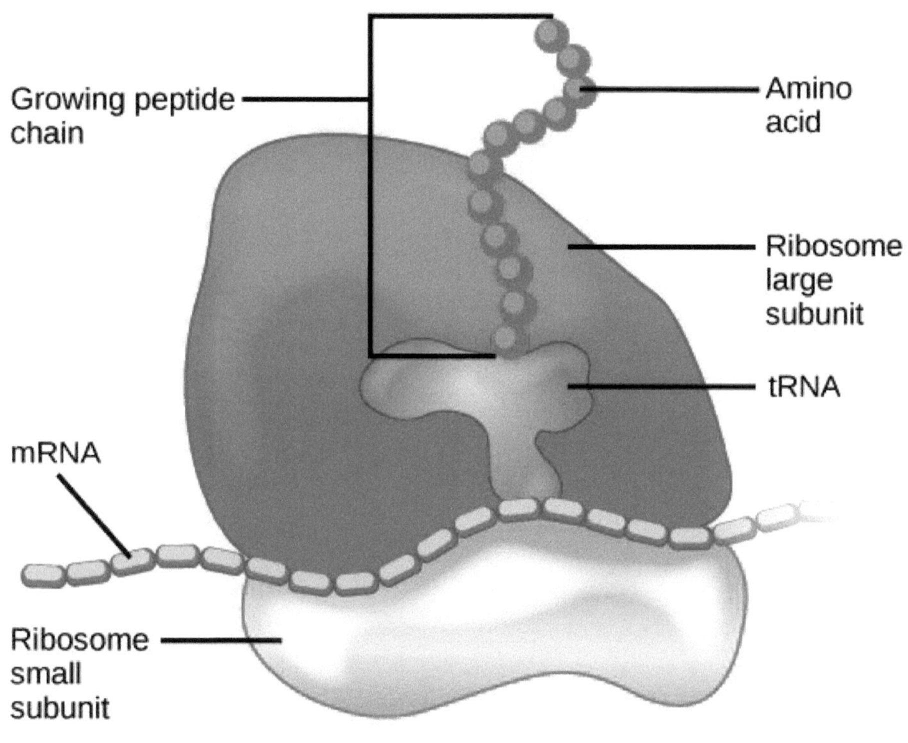

RIBOSOME

- These are porous hydrated and sub-miroscopic organelles which are called as protein factory of the cell or Engine of the cell.
- It is a membrane less smallest organelle.
- To maintain it's structure an increased concentration of Mn(di positive) is required.
- It is spheroid structure which is composed of two sub-units, the upper smaller one and the lower larger one.The upper one is cap shaped and the lower one is dome shaped.
- Claude first observed ribosome and called them Mesosomes.
- Palade in 1953 discovered and named ribosomes.
- They are also called as Palade particles.
- Made of proteins & rRNA, So also called as RNA particles.
- They are not true organelles.
- They are universal.
- Present in both Eukaryotes and Prokaryotes.
- Some ribosomes are present in mitochondria (mitoribosomes) and plastids (plastidoribosomes). Because of this nature they are called as organelles within organelles.
- Number varies from cell to cell i.e 10000 - 30000 in bacterial cell & 2-10 million in mamallian cell.

classification

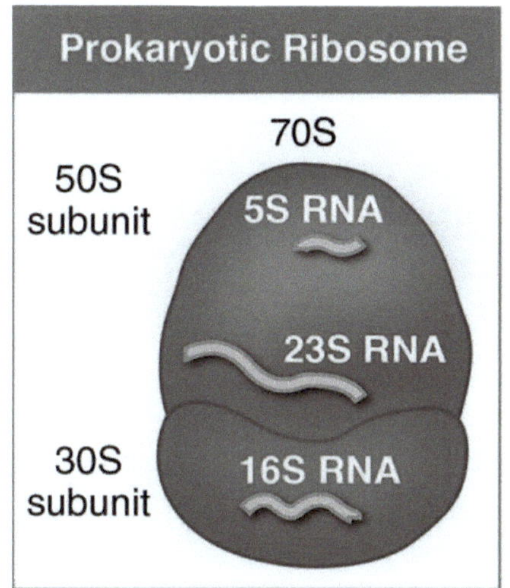

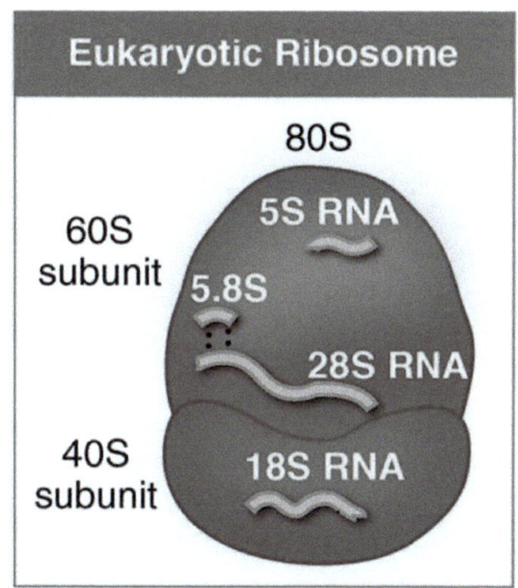

TYPES OF RIBOSOMES

70S RIBOSOMES

- Smaller subunit Contain 21 types of proteins .
- Larger subunit Contain 34 types of proteins .
- RNA : Protein ratio is 60 : 40
- Molecular mass = 2.7-3 megadalton
- Inhibited by Chlorophenical

80S RIBOSOMES

- Smaller subunit Contain 30 types of proteins .
- Larger subunit Contain 40 types of proteins.
- RNA : Protein = 40 : 60
- Inhibited by Cyclohexamide

5S rRNA helps in recognising tRNA during protein synthesis and is common to both 70s and 80s ribosomes.

In Prokaryotes ribosomes may be isolated or may be attached to single mRNA known as Polysome/Ergasome/Polyribosome. It leads to Translational amplication(protein synthesis).

In Eukaryotes ribosomes may be free in the cytoplasm or may be attached to nuclear membrane or endoplasmic reticulum with the help of Ribophorin 1 and Ribophorin 2. Larger subunit is attached to ER or nuclear membrane.

BIOGENESIS OF RIBOSOME

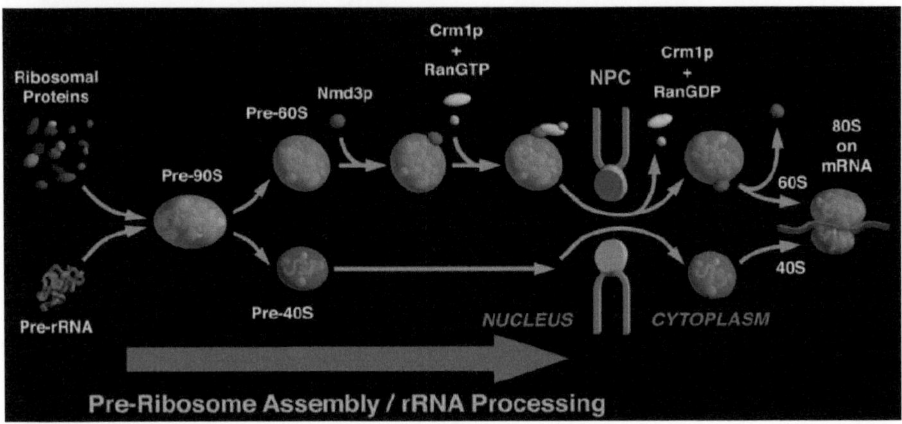

BIOGENESIS OF RIBOSOME

- In prokaryotes it occus inside the cytoplasm.
- In eukaryotes it occurs inside nucleus in a structure called as nucleolus. After the formation of ribosomes these are transferred to the cytoplasm where they mature.

IMPORTANT POINTS ABOUT RIBOSOME

- ***In bean root cells Robinson and Brown observed ribosomes.***
- ***Ribosomes are negatively charged***
- ***They contain two types of proteins***

1. ***Core Proteins required for attachment to mRNA***
2. ***Split proteins act as enzymes and factors during translation***

- According to Lake they are assymmetrical
- Steffer and Whitman proposed Quasi symmetrical model of ribosomes
- Free ribosomes synthesise enzymatic and structural proteins while as bound ribosomes synthesise transport proteins.

VII
MITOCHONDRIA

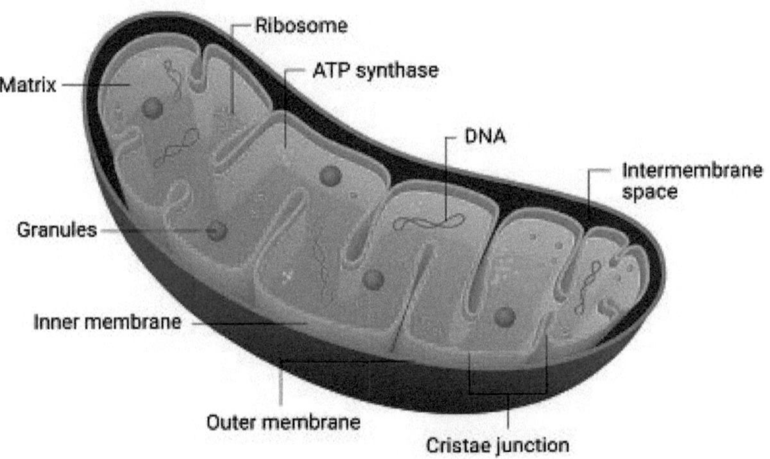

MITOCHONDRIA

- Mitochondria is a double membrane organelle which can be seen under electron microscope as well as optical microscope, when stined with JanusgreenB. It is the largest cytoplasmic organelle in animal cells. In plant cells it is the second largest cytoplasmic organelle, first being the plastid.
- Mitochondria is the site for aerobic respiration and oxidative phosphorylation, which produces ATP. ATP is also called as the biological currency of the cell.
- Mitochondria generates ATP therefore it is also called as ATP mill of the cell, powerhouse of cell or poerbatteries of the cell.

DISCOVERY

- Mitochondria were first observed by Kolliker in flight muscles of insects.These appeared small granules and he called them as Sarcosomes.
- The term mitochondria was coined by Carl Benda.
- Flemming called mitochondria as filia, altman called mitochondria as bioblasts.

SHAPE AND NUMBER

- In most of the cells mitochondria is sausage shape or cylindrical in shape but in case of Chlorella the shape of mitochondria is tubular or branched.
- Number of mitochondria varies from cell to cell depending upon the function of cell or activity of the cell, e.g in Trypanosoma and Chlorella the number of mitochondria inside the cell is one.In flight muscle cells of insects the no. of mitochondria is upto 5 lakh.
- Prokaryotic cells lack mitochondria instead they contain Mesosomes. Mitochondria is present in eukaryotic cells ecxept mature RBCs.
- Length = 1-4 microns
- Breadth = 0.2-1 micron
- Largest mitochondria = Rana Pipiens(20-40 microns).

COMPOSITION

- Proteins = 60-70 %
- Lipids = 25-30 %
- RNA = 5-7 %
- DNA & ions in trace amounts
- Principle Cation = Mn

STRUCTURE

The ultrastructure reveals following components ;-

1. Outer membrane.
2. Outer chamber/Peri-miotochondrial space.
3. Inner membrane.
4. Inner chamber/matrix

OUTER MEMBRANE

- ***Thickness = 65-70 A***
- ***Highly permeable due to presence of porins***
- ***Less cardiolipin***
- ***Protein : Lipid = 60: 40***
- ***Marker enzyme = Monoamine oxidase***
- ***Permeable to substances of molecular weight less than 10000 daltons***

OUTER CHAMBER

- ***Space between outer and inner membrane***
- ***Marker enzyme = Adenylate kinase***
- ***Also known as inter membrane space***

INNER CHAMBER

- ***Contains all the enzymes required for krebs cycle except SUCCINATE DEHYDROGENASE***
- ***Contains ribosomes (70s) and double stranded circular DNA***
- Semi-autonomous organelle as it can synthesise 19 types of tRNA and 12 types of mRNA

INNER MEMBRANE

-

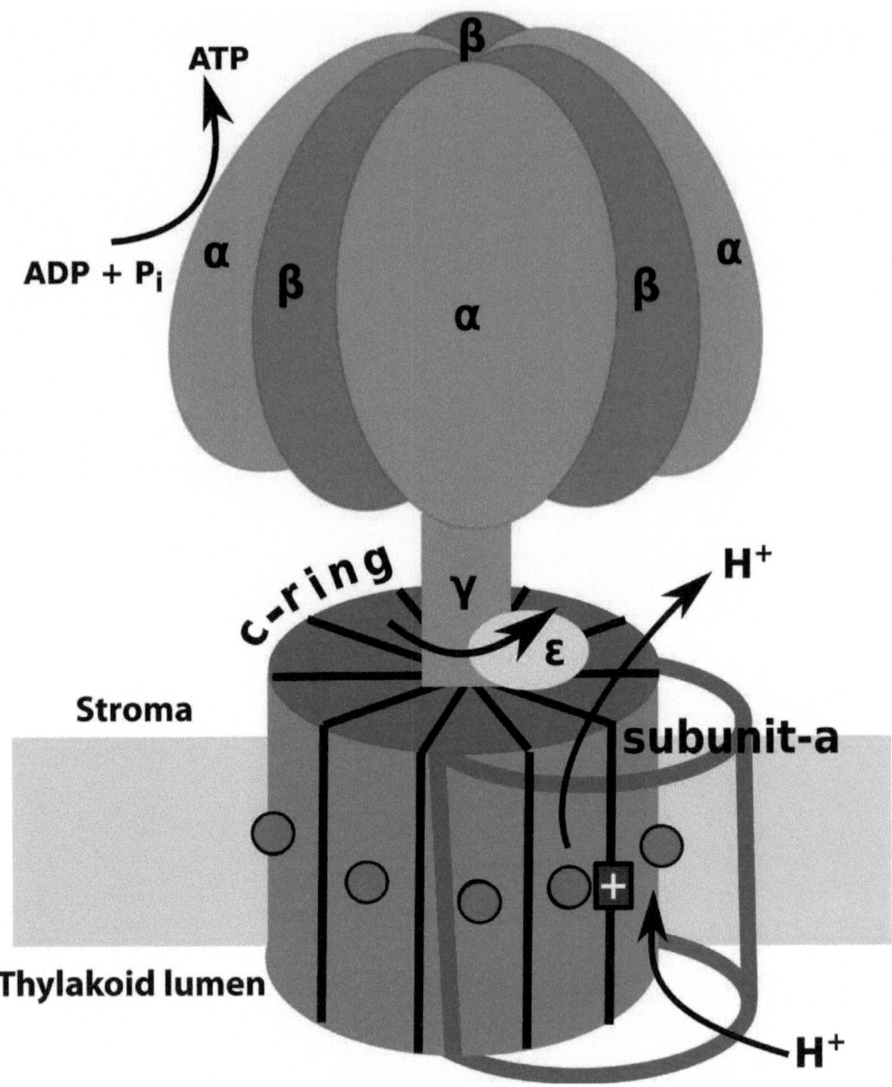

Enter Caption

- ***Thickness = 65-70A***
- ***Marker enzyme = Cytochrome oxidase (important for ETC)***
- ***7 times more Cardiolipns than outer membrane***
- ***Protein : Lipid = 80 : 20***
- Less Porins

- Selectively permeable
- Contain F0-F1 particles

VIII
LYSOSOME

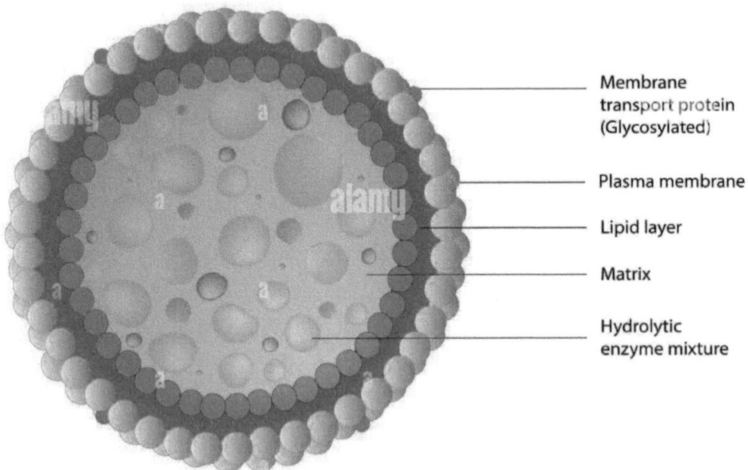

- Lysosomes are small vesicle like single membrane bound organelle which contains digestive or hydrolytic enzymes.
- The enzymes are involved in intra cellular digestion and they act in acidic pH. The lumen of a lysosome is maintained in an acidic pH with the help of of an ATP dependent proton pump which is present in the

wall of a lysosome.
- The proton pump actively pumps the protons from cytoplasm of the cell into the lumen of the lysosome.
- Size = 0.2-0.8 microns
- In monocytes size is 5 microns.
- Marker enzyme = Acid Phosphatase

DISCOVERY

- ***First observed by christian de duve in rat liver cells and he called them as peri-nuclear dense bodies.***
- ***Later on he renamed them as lysosomes***
- ***Ultra structure was studied by Alex Novikoff***
- ***Enzymes of lysosomes are known as Acid hydrolases***

OCCURANCE

- ***Present in animal cells and rarely seen in plant cells***
- ***They are present in maximum concentration in Granulocytes***
- ***Lysosomal activity in plants is shown by Sphaeosomes***

ENZYMES

1. ***GLYCOSIDASE***
2. ***PROTEASE***
3. ***LIPASE***
4. ***NUCLEASE***
5. ***PHOSPHATASE***
6. ***SULPHITASE***

SYNONYMS

- ***SUICIDAL BAG***
- ***ATOM BOMB OF CELL***
- ***SCAVANGER OF CELL***

The membrane of a lysosome contains SIALIC ACID which prevents auto digestion of its own membrane by its own enzymes.

STABLIZERS

Chemicals present in the wall of lysosome that help in stablizing the wall of the lysozome

e g cholesterol , heparin , cortisone & cortisol

LABILIZERS

Chemicals inside the wall of lysosome which disrupt or make the wall instable

e g X-rays , excess amount of vitamin A, D, E, K

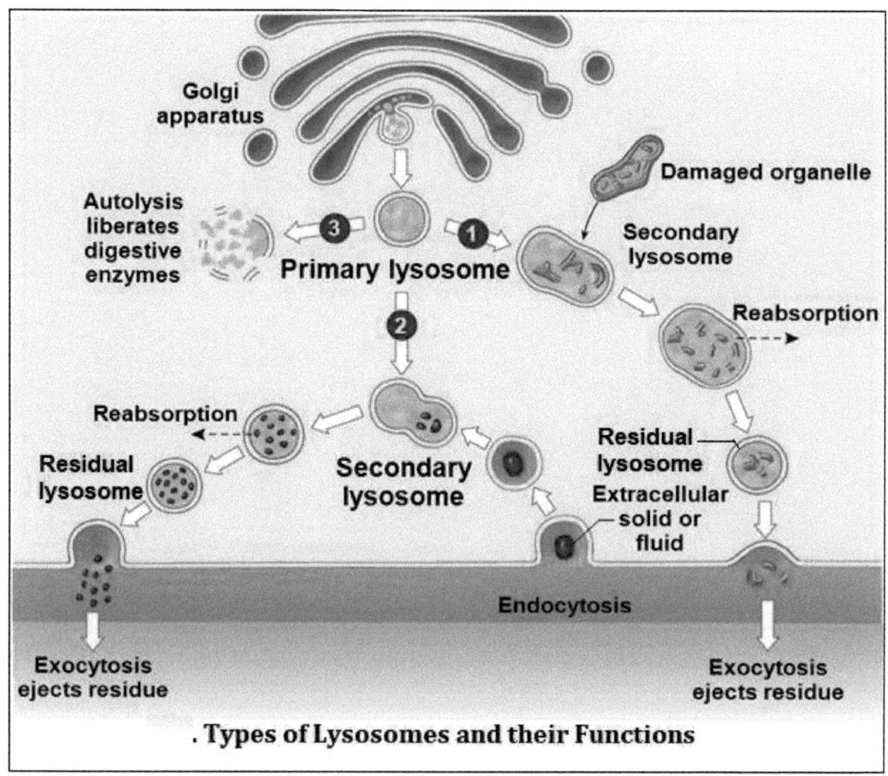

. Types of Lysosomes and their Functions

FUNCTIONS

1. ***Metamorphosis of tadpole***
2. ***Bone formation***
3. ***Intra cellular digestion***
4. ***Digestion of extra cellular substances***
5. ***Immunity***
6. ***Ageing***
7. ***CRINOPHAGY(Act on thyroglobulin to release T3 and T4 from thyroid gland)***

IX
NUCLEUS

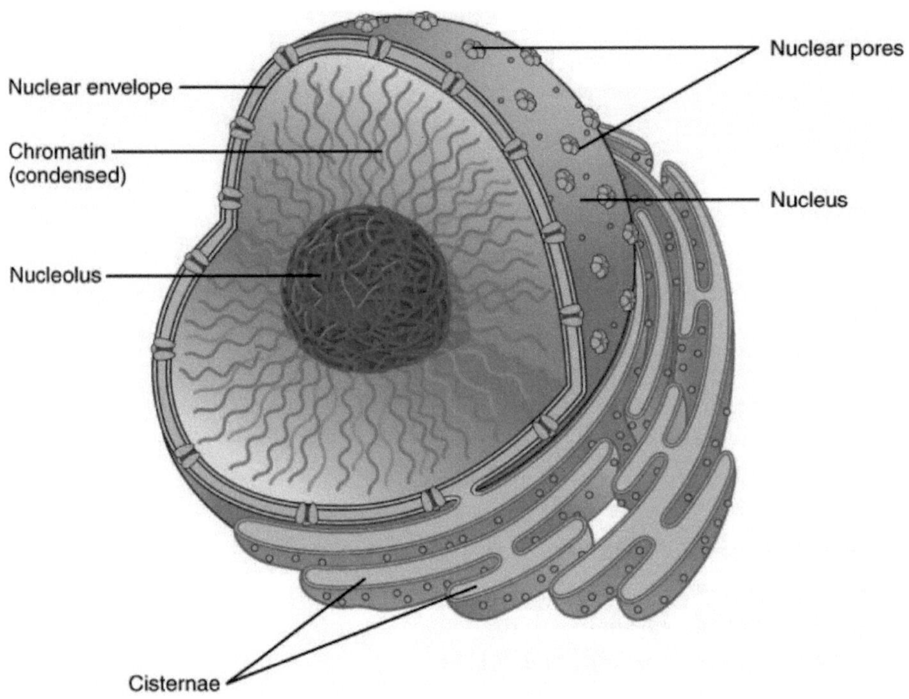

- Nucleus is the largest protoplasmic organelle.It is called as the control centre of the cell or the director of the cell because it stores genetic information and controls the metabolic activities of the cell.

- Most of cells are monokaryotic but their no varies from cell to cell.In RBC there is no nucleus
- Nucleus is centrally placed(cuboidal cells), at base(columnar cells),eccentric(adipocytes)
- Best seen in Interphase

DISCOVERY

- Discovered by Robert Brown in root cells of orchid plant .
- Robert Brown coined the term nucleus.

SHAPE

- ***Cuboidal cells = spherical***
- Columnar cells = elongated
- Epithelial cells = flat
- Paramecium = bean shaped
- Platyphylax = branched
- Neutrophills = multilobed
- Acidophills = bilobed/spectacle shaped

COMPOSITION

- ***Acidic protein = 65 %***
- ***Basic protein = 15 %***
- ***DNA = 12 %***
- ***RNA = 5 %***
- ***Enzymes***
- ***Minerals***

STRUCTURE

1. ***Nuclear Membrane/Karyotheca/Nuclear envelope***
2. ***Nucleoplasm/Karyoplasm***
3. ***Nucleolus***
4. ***Chromatin***

NUCLEAR MEMBRANE

- Discovered by Robert Brown
- Bilayered; outer ecto-karyotheca continuous with ER and bears Ribosomes
- Inner endo-karyotheca contain fibrous proteins
- 60-90A thick
- Formed of lipoproteins
- Cointains nuclear pores which are octagonal in shape responsible for transport of substances
- It covers peri nuclear space (10-50A)

CHROMATIN

- Discovered by Flemming
- ***Made of Proteins, DNA and RNA***
- ***Proteins may be acidic or basic or both***
- Histones are involved in coiling
- ***It is of two types***

1. ***Euchromatin***
2. ***Heterochromatin***

NUCLEOPLASM

- Discovered by Strausberger
- contains enzymes for transcription and translation
- Contains Cajal bodies which are required for synthesis of telomers

NUCLEOLUS

- ***Membrane less structure***
- ***Discovered by FONTANA and studied by WAGNER***
- ***Term coined by BOWMAN***
- ***Formed of RNA & proteins***
- ***Present in NOR***
- ***Ribosomal Factory***
- ***Ca is required for maintaining its structure***

X

PLASTIDS

Internal membrane
Intermembrane space
External membrane
Granum
Plastoglobule
Ribosome
Chloroplast DNA
Stroma
Thylakoid
Lamella
Thylakoid membrane
Lumen

- DISCOVERED BY HAECKEL & SCHIMPER
- They are of three types

1. Leucoplast
2. Chromoplast

3. Chloroplast

LEUCOPLAST

- ***Colourless***
- ***Lacks pigments.***
- ***Storage purpose.***
- ***Largest plastid.***
- ***It is of three types.***

1. Amyloplast: stores starch (potato,rice, wheat)
2. Aleuroplast/Proteinoplast : stores proteins (corn)
3. Lipidoplast/Elioplast: stores lipids (tuberose)

CHROMOPLAST

- Coloured.
- Contain carotenoides and xanthophills.
- Provide colour to flowers and fruits.
- Contain absisic acid involved in seed dormancy, opening and closing of stomata.

CHOLOROPLAST

- Green in colour due to presence of cholorophyll which is involved in photosynthesis.
- Also called kitchen of cell.
- Discovered by Leewenhock & Grew and were studied by Sachs
- Length = 5-10 microns
- Width = 2-5 microns
- They occur in higher plants, Diatoms ,Euglanoids and absent in prokaryotes.

- Disc shaped in plants.
- Collar shaped in Ulothrix.
- Ribbon shaped in Spirogyra.
- Cup shaped in Chyllamadomanas.

COMPOSITION

- ***Proteins = 50-60 %***
- ***Lipids = 20-30 %***
- ***Chlorophyll = 5-10 %***
- ***DNA = 5 %***
- ***RNA = 3 %***
- ***Minerals***
- ***Vitamins***
- ***Pigments***

ULTRASTRUCTURE

1. Envelope
2. Stroma
3. Thylakoids

XI
ENDOPLASMIC RETICULUM

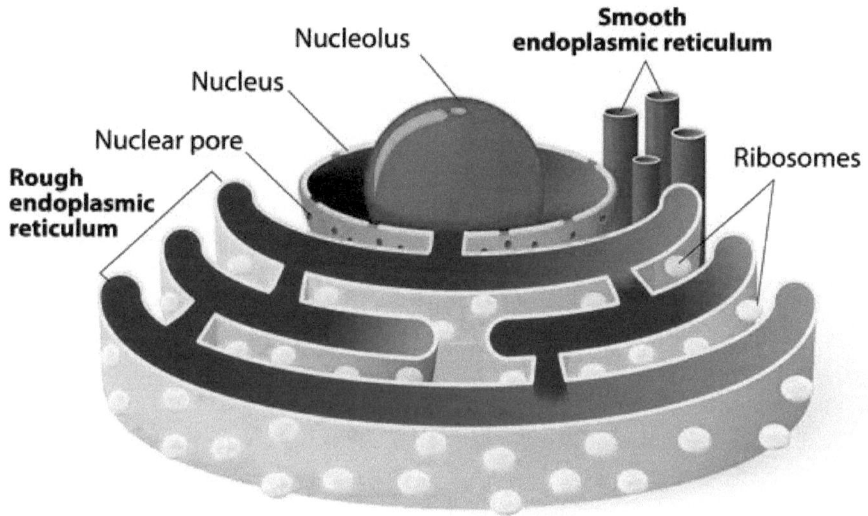

- Garnier hinted the presence of ER through basophillic reactions and called it ergastoplasm

- Porter & Thomson studied its structure under electron microscope
- Porter coined the term ER
- It is a reticulate organelle consisting of Cisternae, Tubules, Vacoules
- ER forms 30-60% of EMS(endomembrane system).
- 40 times more surface area than cell
- Present in eukaryotes except RBC, ovum, early embryonic cells
- Produce membrane of lysosome
- Marker enzyme = cytochrome P-450
- It has single thinnest mimbrane (50-60A)
- It has three parts

1. Cisternae
2. Tubules
3. Vesicles

- It is of two types

1. RER(Rough ER)
2. SER(smooth ER)

FUNCTIONS

- ### *RER*

1. ***Protein synthesis***
2. ***Post translational modification***

- ### *SER*

1. ***LIPOGENESIS***
2. ***XENOBIOSIS***
3. STORE Ca

4. GIVE RISE TI SPHAEROSOMES
5. FORMATION OF GOLGI BODIES
6. GLYCOGENESIS & GLYCOGENOLYSIS
7. RISE TO GOLGI BODIES

XII
GOLGI BODIES

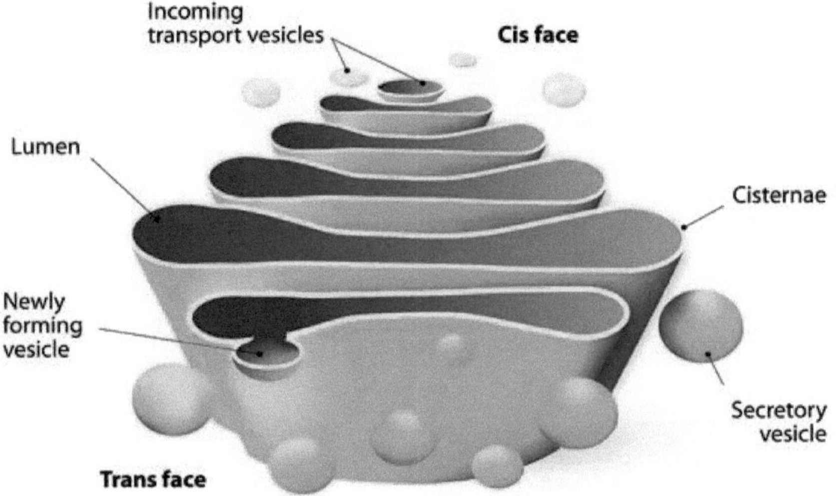

XIII
CELL WALL

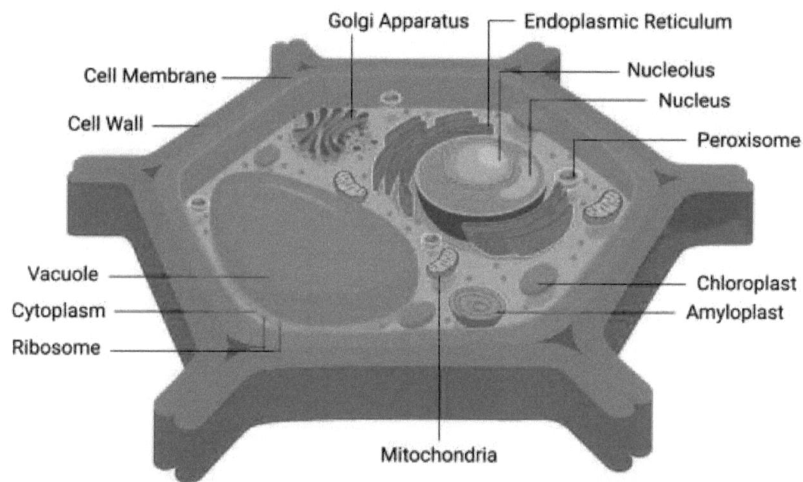

CELL WALL

- It was discoverd by Robert Haoke in1665 in cork cells.
- It is a semi-transparent layer around plasma-membrane and is meant for mechanical support and also provides shape to the plant cell.
- It provides rigidity to the plant cell.
- It is composed of four layers:-

1. Middle lamella
2. Primary wall
3. Secondary wall
4. Teritary wall

XIV
BIOLOGICAL MEMBRANE

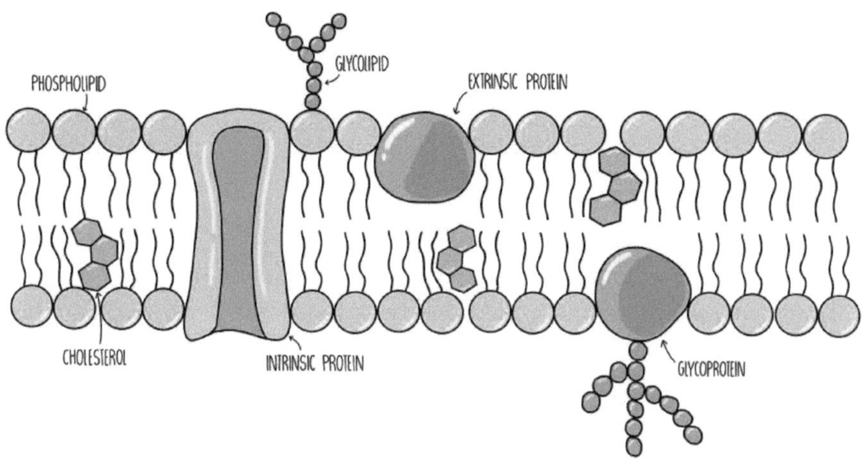

- It is also known as Biomembrane.
- It includes cell membrane as well asorganelle membranes.
- These are made up of biomolecules like proteins , lipids an d carbohydrates.
- Decomposition of biological membrane varies from cell to cell and from organelle to organelle.

PROTEINS

- On the basis of function there are three main types of proteins.

1. Structural protein
2. Functinal protein
3. Transport protein

- On the basis of position/location proteins may be extrinsic or intrinsic.

LIPIDS

- There are various types of lipids in biological membrane but the mostimportant ones are Phospholipids.These are amphiphatic i.e these possess both hydrophilic as well as hydrophobic parts or ends.

CARBOHYDRATES

- They are present on the outer surface of biomembranes and may be of following types:-

1. Fucose
2. Sialic acid
3. Galactose(Brain sugar)

Carbohydrates are essential for maintaining the retentivity of the cell.

MODELS OF BIOLOGICAL MEMBRANE

- There are three models

1. Lipid model
2. Sandwich model
3. Fluid mosaic model

LIPID MODEL

- There are two lipid models

1. Overtons model
2. Gorter & Grindel model.

OVERTONS MODEL

- According to this model a biological membrane is made up of lipids because lipids pass freely through a membrane.

GORTER & GRINDEL'S MODEL

- According to this model a biological membrane is made up of lipids and the surface area of lipids is twice the surface area of the cell

SANDWICH MODEL

This model includes Lamellar model and Robert Sonian unit membrane model.

LAMELLAR MODEL

Sandwich (Davson–Danielli) model of cell membrane

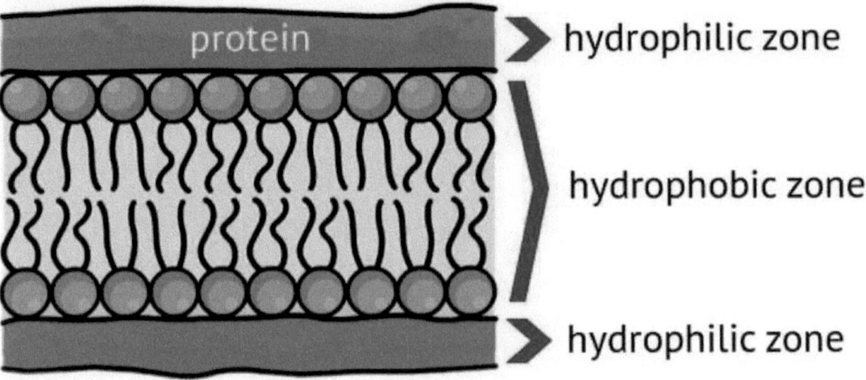

- This model was given by Daneilliand Davson .
- According to this model a phospholipid bilayer is sandwiched between Alpha-hydrated globular proteins.Thus the biomembrane is tri-laminar.

ROBERTSONIAN UNIT MEMBRANE MODEL

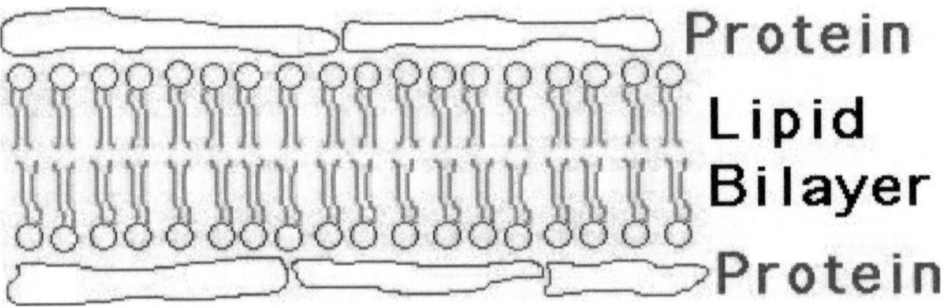

- According to this model a phospholipid bilayer is sandwiched betweeen two layers of Beta-extended proteins

FLUID MOSAIC MODEL

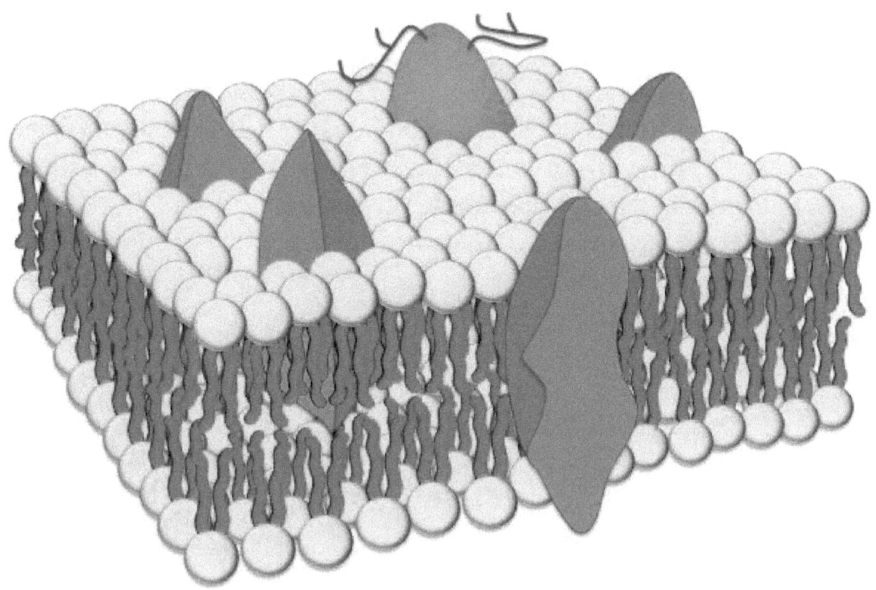

- This model was given by Singer and Nicholson in 1972. It is a dynamic model because various cellular processess like endocytosis, exocytosis, pinocytosis, growth and cybrid formation can be explained through this model.
- According to this model, a biomembrane consists of a phospholipid bilayer. The phospholipid molecules possess a hydrophilic head which is directed outwards and a tail which is hydrophoibic and is directed inwards thus the phopholipid bilayer podssess tail to tail arrangement. The outer phospholipid layer is formed of cephalin and the inner one is made up of lecithi.Proteins according to position /location may be divided into two types i.e Extrinsic and Intrinsic proteins.
-

Extrinsic protein

- Also called as peripheral proteins because they are located on the inner and outer sides of the membrane. The constitute about 30% of the protein content.These proteins cam be easily separated with Sonication.
-

Intrinsic proteins

- Also called as integral proteins because they are present within the membrane .They constitue about 70% of the protein content.It is difficult to separate the intrinsic proteins through sonication.The integral protein that passes through the entire thickness of the membrane called as channel protein which helps in water transport.
- Carbohydrates are presnt on the outer surface of the membrane. These may combine with lipids to form glycolipids or they combine with proteins to form glycoproteins.

XV
CENTRIOLE

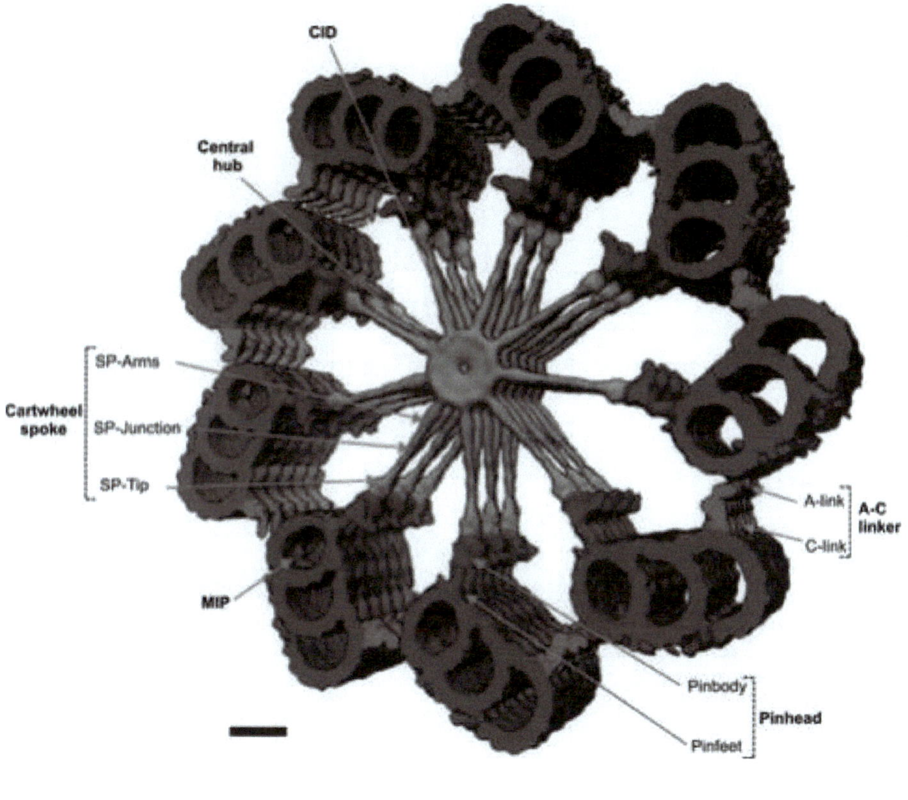

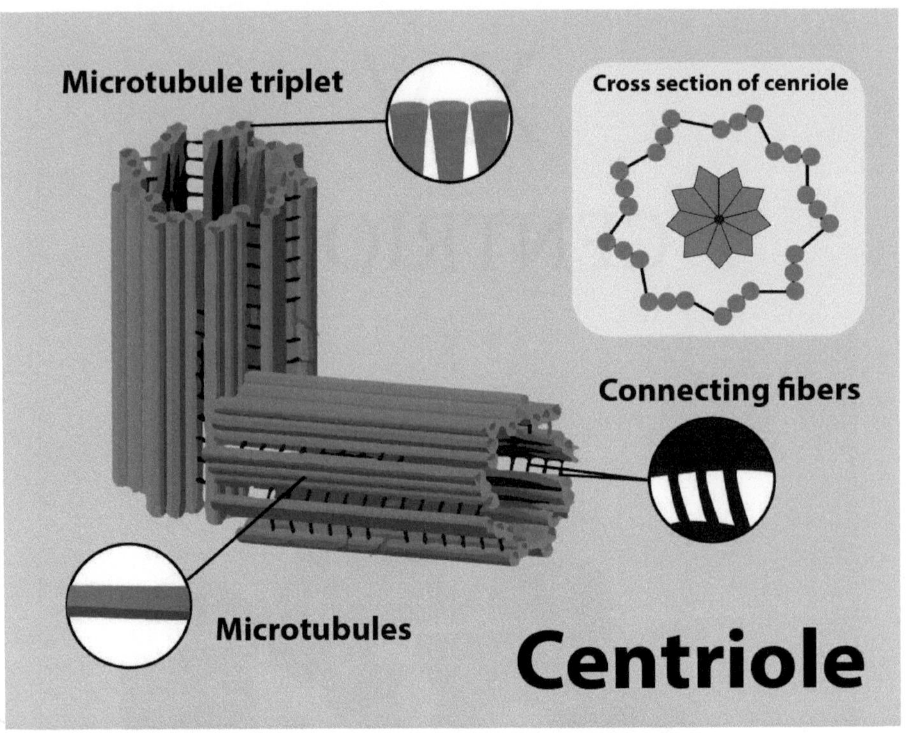

- They are present in eukaryotic animal cell while as higher plants lack centrioles.
- They are sub microscopic cylinders which are placed perpendicular to each other in pairs
- A paired structure of centrioles is known as a DIPLOSOME
- The cytoplasm around diplosome is devoid of organells and is called as CENTROPHORE/ZONE OF EXCULSION
- Dicovered by Boveri
- DIPLOSOME + CENTROSPHERE = CENTROSOME

XVI
CILIA AND FLAGELLA

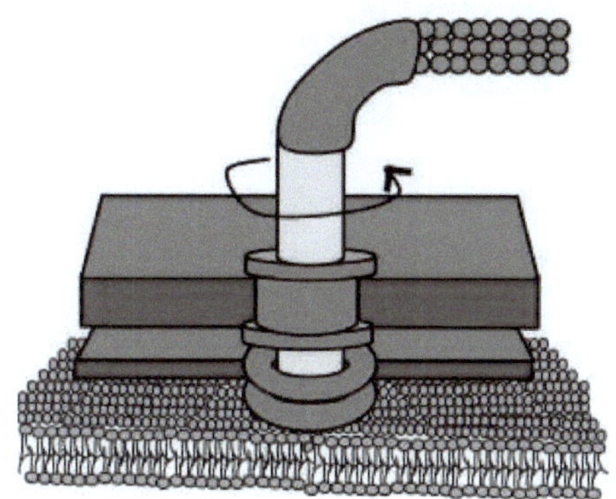

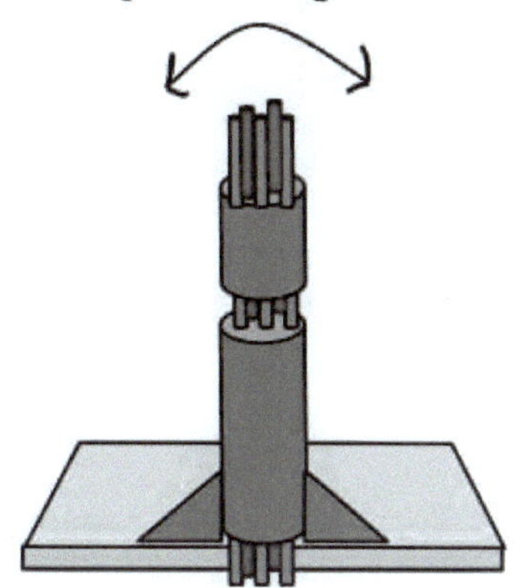

FLAGELLA

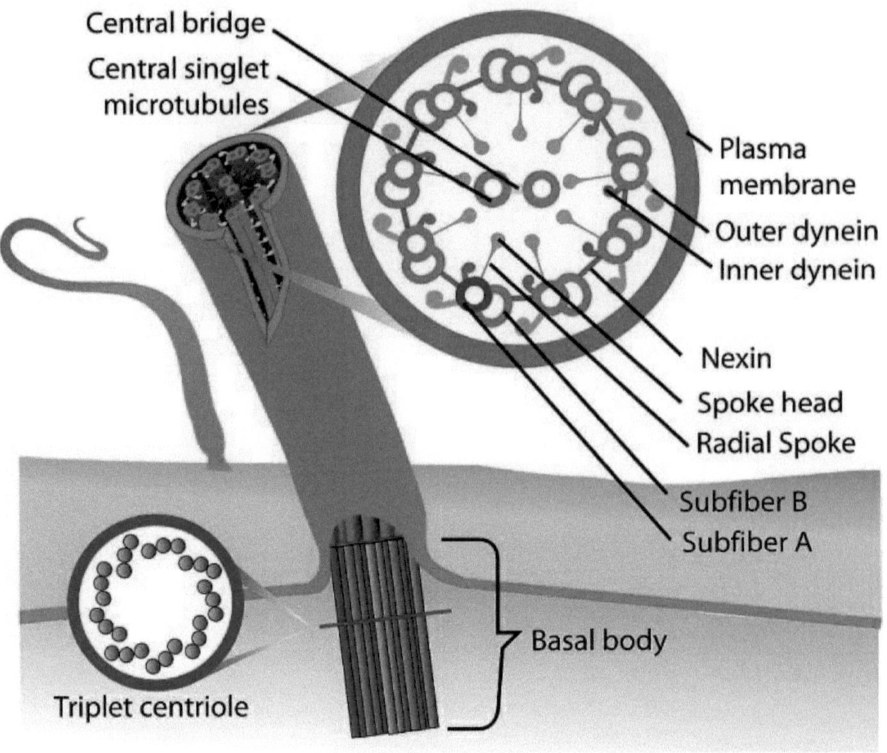

CILIA

- These are microscopic outgrowths which are contractile in nature and can function as sensory organs as well as organs of locomotion
- These werwe discovered by Engelman
- It contains following structure

1. Kinetosome/Basal body
2. Rootlets
3. Basal Plate
4. Shaft

XVII
VACOULE

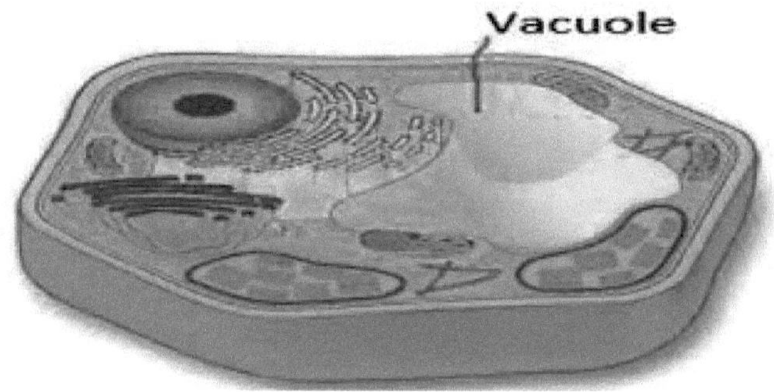

- It is a non cytoplasmic region in the cytoplasm which is provided with specific membrane
- It is of following types

1. SAP VACOULE
2. CONTRACTILE VACOULE
3. FOOD VACOULE
4. GAS VACOULE

WORDS OF THANKS

THANKS TO ALL READERS

YOU CAN DROP ALL YOUR SUGGESTIONS AT

E mail : hanannaikoo@protonmail.com

9 798885 556323

Printed by Libri Plureos GmbH in Hamburg,
Germany